Planning Quality Project Management of (EMR/EHR) Software Products

Planning Quality Project Management of (EMR/EHR) Software Products

By

Richard L. Chamberlain, PhD

CRC Press
Taylor & Francis Group
Boca Raton London New York

CRC Press is an imprint of the
Taylor & Francis Group, an **informa** business

A PRODUCTIVITY PRESS BOOK

CRC Press
Taylor & Francis Group
6000 Broken Sound Parkway NW, Suite 300
Boca Raton, FL 33487-2742

© 2018 by Richard L. Chamberlain
CRC Press is an imprint of Taylor & Francis Group, an Informa business

No claim to original U.S. Government works

Printed on acid-free paper

International Standard Book Number-13: 978-1-138-31020-9 (Hardback)
International Standard Book Number-13: 978-1-138-31018-6 (Paperback)
International Standard Book Number-13: 978-1-315-14364-4 (eBook)

Visit the Taylor & Francis Web site at
http://www.taylorandfrancis.com

and the CRC Press Web site at
http://www.crcpress.com

Dedication

Dedicated to friends I work with

to contribute to Health Care

Contents

Acknowledgments

I want to thank my daughters and their families.

I received encouragement from them and numerous other people as I prepared this. I wish to thank them all.

The "sayings" at the beginning of each chapter are from the website: http://www.devrand.com/.

Chapter 1

Introduction: The Basics

Patient Safety

We are going to be discussing the implementation and support of computer systems used for managing patient medical information.

We will first cover some notions related to quality that are very important to the treatment of patients, including topics such as

Quality
Quality Assurance
Quality Management

We will then go through the steps of implementation and use of a computer system (the plan) and how quality is incorporated into the implementation.

Whenever this is done here or in other documents the number one concern is always patient safety.

Is anything happening that could negatively affect the safety of the patient or make the patient safer?

Even if a related topic is being examined, like the cost of doing an MRI, the safety of the patient for each cost alternative could be considered.

We will consider patient safety throughout our discussions here.

Quality

The safety of the patient will inevitably be a function of the quality of the procedures used to manage their information and the procedures used to see and treat the patient.

Since we are talking about quality management, quality is very important.

There is a point regarding quality that is often overlooked. That point is that to really do quality management you and almost everyone in the organization has to live and breathe quality.

Quality has to be a way of life. It has to permeate almost everything and everyone. This is based on actual history by the icons of quality.

During W.E. Deming's time, there was a notion that quality was P-D-C-A, where the letters stand for the following.

Plan–Do–Check–Act

The idea is that you *Plan* what you are going to do, then you *Do* it according to that plan. Then, you *Check* it to see whether it is all correct and *Act* based on what you see.

Deming referred to this as a "corruption." He said it should be P-D-S-A. Where you *Plan* what you are going to do, then you *Do* it according to that plan. Then you *Study* it to see whether you really are doing things the best way, and then *Act* based on what you see. Essentially, there is more to it than just checking. You need to really consider everything you are doing to see whether there is not a better way.

Throughout his work he tried to implant quality throughout an organization.

He is also well known for his 14 points that he considered the basis for "Profound Knowledge." See Appendix A.

One can tell by these "Key Principles" that quality is the way you do things.

There is another reference, *Well Made in America*, which is the story of the recovery of Harley Davidson. Harley Davidson almost went out of business in the 1970s. It was bought by AMF (the bowling people). After a couple of years, about a dozen managers in AMF raised some money, bought Harley Davidson back, and took it public. At the same time they decided to improve the quality of the bikes. The quality of the bikes was really bad. They said one year the paint jobs were so bad that as people walked by them in the show room, the air would make the paint flake off and fall on the floor. They also said that 50% of the bikes coming off the assembly line would not start.

They went through a lot of effort and now Harley Davidson motor bikes are arguably some of the highest quality bikes on the market. (I know because I own one.)

In the book above, AMF said they attributed the success of increasing the quality of their bikes to three things.

The first was called *EI*, or Employee Involvement. They found that they had to involve everyone in the increase of quality. You cannot assign quality to a focus group in the corner and everyone else keeps on working.

The second was *JIT*, Just In Time, which was an inventory procedure. The problem was that 50% of the materials they were receiving from their suppliers were bad. So what do you do in that situation? They ordered twice as much as they needed and were building huge, worthless inventories. Essentially, they had a lot of bad procedures.

The third thing to which they attributed their success was Statistical Quality Control. The one thing they said they did wrong was, they implement Quality Control (QC) last when they should have done it first.

One definition of the word quality is: producing or providing products or services of high quality or merit.

Much of this notion carries over into the International Organization for Standardization (ISO) and some other standards such as, World Health Organization (WHO), IEEE Software Engineering Standards, American College of Physicians, and the Project Management Institute Body of Knowledge (PMIBOK).

That is, quality involves everyone. It has to become a way of life for it to be effective. It is not something you can assign to a group in the corner.

Auditing

Auditing is a very important component of quality and compliances and a few other issues we are discussing here. Under a 1994 standard [1] and some other documents, the auditing process could be adequately addressed by performing the following compliance auditing:

■ Tell me what you are supposed to do (describe the business process)
■ Show me where that is written (reference the procedure manuals)
■ Prove that is what happened (exhibit evidence in documented records)
■ Is this the best you can do?

These steps are basically an audit. Auditing is a very important part of quality assurance.

Most of the discussions of quality will include the phrase, *the ability to demonstrate*. In other words, there has to be documentation or some other kind of product to show that you are operating according to certain rules or regulations when you do the *Study* step. It can be very difficult if there is nothing to study.

These rules typically generate a series of steps derived to make it possible for us to follow the rules and produce the desired product. Many of us follow good business practices. The regulatory bodies will argue that the regulations are just good business practice. In any case, there is a need for an underlying process that has been defined and that we try to follow, and this process is defined to have us satisfy any business or regulatory requirements; thus, the need for the processes we have been discussing.

When we have a series of steps that we follow, the questions can be asked: *Are you following the process?*, *Are you producing the desired product?*, and *Can you show that you are?*.

One good way to show you are following the process and producing the desired result is to use quality assurance (QA) practices.

A recommendation: fairly early in becoming compliant, your group should sit down and compile a list of the business practices you are expected to follow and if necessary, any regulations that might apply.

It should become obvious that one of the functions of the ISO 9000 is to show that quality is built in to what you are doing; it is a way of doing things.

Quality Management

Before getting into quality management, it is important to lay out some practice and procedures that have to be understood which form the basis for quality management.

Quality management is quality that is applied to processes. In many cases, these processes are not well-defined or well-understood.

Quality management is a very broad area. Although not the only guidance on quality management, certainly one of the most referenced is ISO 9000. There is extensive documentation on how to apply it and it has its own set of documents that refine or expand on the different parts of the standard.

Even the Food and Drug Administration (FDA), in the document, *The Food and Drug Administration Safety and Innovation Act (FDASIA)*, emphasizes that quality management is required in Electronic Health Records (EHR) systems instead of requiring regulations.

See FDASIA in Appendix B for the following.

The application of quality management principles, including a quality systems approach by health IT stakeholders, is necessary for the safe design, development, implementation, customization, and use of health IT. The Agencies will work with health IT stakeholders to identify the essential elements of a health IT quality framework, leveraging existing quality management principles and identifying areas where quality management principles can or should be applied. The agencies view this strategy, rather than a formal regulatory approach, as the appropriate method for advancing a health IT quality framework.

Therefore, this document will use ISO 9000 as the focal point for its recommendations for quality management. However, it will include references to other efforts that are consistent with ISO 9000, but might be more specific for the computer systems being discussed here.

Documentation

Perhaps the one underlying rule in everything we do here is that there must be documentation.

The key to quality (and some of the other things we do) is documentation.

There is a companion document to the ISO 9000 that describes the requirements of ISO documentation:

Document ISO/TC 176/SC 2/N 525R2
Guidance on the Documentation Requirements of
   ISO 9001:2008

When I studied for my PhD, my Major Professor asked me to prove a theorem. My Major Professor was a fairly well known statistician named Oscar Kempthorne.

He was having a dispute with a colleague at the time. I could see how, if the theorem was true, his colleague was wrong. I spent a year trying to prove that theorem; then one day, the light went on and I wondered whether perhaps the theorem was not true. I had done enough research that I came up with a counter example to show the theorem was not true and I could see a year's worth of research and my PhD going down the drain. Anyway, the research I had been doing also showed me how to rewrite the theorem so it was true and fortunately for me it still showed his colleague was wrong.

So I documented my findings and set up a meeting with Kempthorne and walked him through it. When I finished, he leaned back in his chair, looked out the window, and then turned to me and said, "You know, Dick, the written word is very *unreliable*." Then he leaned in so he was right in my face and said, "*but it is the only thing we have.*" He was telling me to write it up, and a few months later I was finished.

But he was absolutely right. The documentation trail, products, and other trails we leave after our work is "the only thing we have!"

The questions become:

What documentation do we need?
How do we generate the documentation?
How do we assure that the documentation is accurate?
How do we store and retrieve the documentation?
Is there some documentation that is not necessary or redundant?
Do we have to generate a new document or can we reference another document?
And others.

As we get into processes and quality, the answers to these questions will become clearer.

The definition of document in the ISO 9000:2005 clause 3.7.2 gives the following examples:

■ Paper
■ Magnetic
■ Electronic or optical computer disc
■ Photograph
■ Master sample

If you work in an environment where there is no documentation, or if you believe you can do quality and compliance without documentation, we would recommend that you get into a different business.

Need for Documentation

What are you supposed to do?
What do you produce that you can touch?
   Proof of the process
   Proof of the product
Who is responsible?
Is everyone trained?

The above needs are all things we do as we see patients. They all become vital as we use the computer to manage the patients' information and their care.

Chapter 2

Quality Management

We are about to implement what we are calling a process to produce something. You might call this something else. That is perfectly all right as long as you produce definitions and are consistent.

These words are used to be consistent with the terms used in ISO 9000.

There are four words that are used in what we are about to do; that is, define our processes and then what make up the processes that we use. It is vital that you and your organization have your own definitions for these words. It will also be important for you to understand how they map to similar words in the various business practices, regulations, guidance documents, and other documentation.

The four words are

Project
Process
Procedure
Product

In all four cases, we will be using the noun version of these words.

The projects we are defining will be made up of processes and procedures that produce products.

If you use the Internet and search these four words you will find a large variety of definitions. In one case, it says, "There are 190 definitions of the word Project."

Based on that, the following definitions have been chosen for use here.

> Project: A temporary endeavor undertaken to create a unique product or service
> Process: A series of actions or steps taken in order to achieve a particular end.
> Procedure: A particular course or mode of action.
> Product: A good, idea, method, information, object, or service created as a result of a process, project, or procedure and serves a need or satisfies a want.

The Projects

The projects are endeavors undertaken to create a unique product, service, or procedure. Some of the projects will be temporary and produce a single result and then are closed. Other projects, such as the development of a computer system, will likely have a maintenance and support phase with procedures that will exist for the life of the system.

Interfacing to some laboratory instruments might be a separate project.

The Processes

At the top, we have processes. These will typically be high-level descriptions of what is to be done. A process might also be called a policy.

We should be able to divide the workload into a set of processes that are performed—the *Divide and Conquer* concept. Sometimes this can be a challenge, but for this discussion most should come from the steps you use to implement your computer system(s).

Some of our processes might be simple cases where there are a handful of simple steps. In other cases, our process might have sub-processes.

There will also be the case that some of the processes have dependencies between them where, for example, one has to finish before another can start.

It is important to develop an understanding of the processes and their relationships when you start to follow them.

The Procedures

The procedures are a series of documented steps to produce a desired product. Similar to projects, there will, in general, be two types of procedures:

■ Continuous procedures
■ Single result procedures

Continuous procedures are those that involve a series of steps that are simply executed in a given situation. For example, seeing a patient should be something that involves a series of steps that are known and documented and are executed each time a patient is seen. The procedure will produce a set of products (results), which should be stored and maintained.

A single result procedure is one that is intended to produce a product that can be used in the process, producing a procedure that is needed for the process. For example, this might be a computer system for something such as reporting serious adverse events. Procedures should describe how to develop and implement a computer system that will support a process for reporting serious adverse events. This project will produce products that are required to support the process.

The above project will go on for the life of the system. It will be necessary to maintain the system as changes are required over the life of the system. There will be projects that have a much shorter life. For example, an unexpected event might happen that requires a project to address the event. This might involve doing something in Excel or Statistical Analysis System (SAS) to obtain the required answer. Once the result is obtained and completed, the project would end.

Note: Obviously, there are other terms that could be used and other ways of interpreting those terms. If a different set of terms is more suited to your organization, business practices, or regulations you should feel free to make the necessary modifications.

Keep in mind that there has to be documentation that describes the steps defined above and those steps need to leave evidence of what actually is done. Without documentation, proof that you are following the steps is impossible.

The Products

In the end, the output of the process will be products that are required for business practices (e.g., Quality Assurance [QA]) or regulations. For example, the output might be documentation, which describes some aspect of the product, or documented evidence, which describes something occurring in a certain way.

In between the projects and the products will be two things: processes and procedures. The procedures will be a more detailed description of what the products are and how to produce them.

Applying these terms in the quality management context is as follows.

A quality management system is simply the quality organization you have, the responsibilities of each part of it, along with names of the managers of the various functions that deliver the desired quality. It will include the quality control (QC) and quality assurance (QA) procedures used to ensure the desired level of quality. It should show how each person has the opportunity to positively influence the quality of what is done.

Quality management suggests that your organization have a quality manual. There is a template for such a document [2]. Toward the end of that template there is a diagram that describes the documentation used in quality management.

Figure 2.1 is a slight variation of that diagram.

The contents of this pyramid are

Quality Manual: This is a document that describes the company's quality organization. A template is available [3].
Policies: Generally, policies are 1–2 pages of high level, standard and somewhat obvious commitment to a concept. In our case they could correspond to processes.

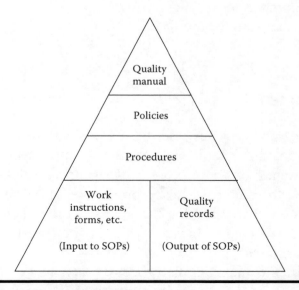

Figure 2.1   Quality management tools.

Procedures: The Standard Operating Procedures, Standard Operating Procedures (SOPs) are a more detailed discussion explaining how to implement the policies/processes.

Below the above three entries there tends to be two types of documents [1]:

1. Documents that form the input to the procedures, such as work practices, manuals, operator's guides, templates, or other more detailed documentation.
2. The output from the procedures—the deliverables. These are also referred to as quality records. These are the documents that will be audited against the other documents.

The quality manual describes the quality organization you have, the responsibilities of each part of it, along with names of the managers of the various functions that deliver the desired quality. It will demonstrate the relationships between the quality organization, for example the quality assurance unit (QAU) and the other parts of the organization. It needs to show the independence of the QAU.

See the template for the Quality Manual.

The Policies

The policies will typically refer to any business requirements or regulations the organization needs to comply with. These it says, these are typically short and leave the detail for the procedures. In some cases, each procedure will have a policy statement near the beginning that refers to the policy the SOP is designed to meet. In this case you may not need separate policy documents.

Procedures come from the processes described earlier. The requirement for QA is to demonstrate that

The processes are being followed.

The processes used and the products produced by the processes meet the required specifications and quality attributes.

So far, the groundwork has been laid out to show that these procedures are what you are doing.

If we look at ISO 9000, it calls for specific activities for documentation.

Requirements for ISO 9000 Documentation

Table 2.1 lists terms and definitions taken from ISO 9000:2005.

Table 2.1   ISO 9000 Documentation – Appendix A

Terms	ISO 9000:2005 Clause	Definition
Document	3.7.2	Information and its supporting medium
Procedure	3.4.5	Specified way to carry out an activity or a process (Note: Procedures can be documented or not)
Quality Manual	3.7.4	Document specifying the quality management system of an organization
Quality Plan	3.7.5	Document specifying which procedures and associated resources shall be applied by whom and when to a specific project, product, process or contract
Record	3.7.6	Document stating results achieved or providing evidence of activities performed
Specification	3.7.3	Document stating requirements

Chapter 3

Managing Patient Information

Observing Patient Information

Patient information can be seen as involving two separate but related things. The first involves the computer system that is used to record and report the patient's medical information.

The other is the observation of the medical information before it is recorded. Many publications that describe patient treatment seem to start when the medical professional has a value ready to enter in the computer. This is not the case! It really starts *when the patient walks in the door.*

Observing the medical information is done by a medical professional that is seeing the patient. Virtually all of this information requires some kind of instrument to make the observation. In some cases a sample is taken and sent to a lab where professionals run the sample through an instrument that might be interfaced to the computer where the value goes directly to the patient's record.

When the medical professional is using an instrument, the following questions are relevant:

Does the instrument need to be calibrated?

Does the instrument need batteries?

Does the medical professional need to be trained?

One major question is, how accurate are the observed values?

If erroneous values are being entered into the computer system, that is something that needs to be known. Some of the computer systems have built-in edit checks that can look for errors. For example, has a value changed more than is possible or practical from the previous visit?

Figure 3.1, shows three components to managing patient information. There can be more components outside of these that do additional processing of a patient's medical information. They should also have quality as a requirement.

The double-sided arrows represent interfaces between the user and the computer system(s). Do the user procedures for collecting and observing the data match the computer systems? If not, can the user procedures be changed or does the computer system need to be changed?

We are focusing on the EMR/EHR systems but there are likely other systems as well, particularly in labs, supporting X-rays, MRIs, or other instruments. Presumably some of these systems might be "interfaced" directly to the EMR/EHR system.

- Do written procedures exist for observing the medical information, taking a sample to send to a lab, or going to a lab for x-rays or other procedures?
- Are these procedures approved and signed off by the medical authority for the practice?
- Are the procedures readily available for the medical professionals that are using them? Are they within reach or are they stored in a library or other document storage location?
- Could copies of these procedures be on a tablet that most of the medical professionals have these days?

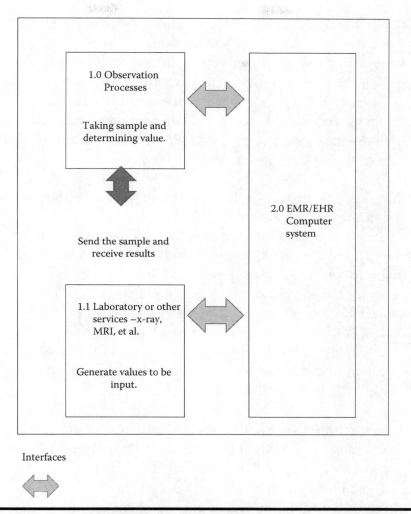

Figure 3.1 EMR/EHR information flow.

Applying Quality Management

W.E. Deming

He said quality assurance is P-D-S-A, where you

■ *Plan* what you are going to do—work out what needs to be done and then prepare procedures to follow.

- *Do* it according to that plan. Follow the procedures to produce the desired results (products).
- *Study* it to see whether you really are doing things the best way. Periodically review what is being done to see whether it is right or whether there is a better way.
- *Act* based on what you see. Based on what the study finds, make a Corrective And Preventative Action (CAPA) plan to implement the desired changes.

You need to really consider everything you are doing to see whether there is a better way.

If procedures like these are not being followed and you cannot know the quality of the data being observed then it is difficult to know the quality of the EMR/EHR system.

The vendor might know the quality of the EMR/EHR system, assuming all of the data being entered was 100% accurate, but that is only part of the answer.

The quality of the information used to treat the patient will be a function of the quality of the three systems mentioned above:

1. Meeting the patient and obtaining the necessary medical information, and then passing that information to the next resource.
2. The lab, X-ray, MRI, or other support function and passing the resulting information to the next resource.
3. The EMR/EHR system and all of its interfaces for storing the information and then retrieving it.

The quality of the information in the EMR/EHR system cannot be better than the quality of the information in the first two resources.

Chapter 4

Applying the Organization to Observation Processes

Defining the Processes

You can define the processes as broadly as you think necessary. For example, some processes might be as follows:

- Implement a computer system for tracking all serious adverse events.
- Implement a process for budgeting and tracking costs and resources for all projects in the company or division of a company.
- Conduct a clinical trial on Drug X.
- Record all necessary medical information when seeing a patient—whatever manual or computer systems might be necessary. Include not only the observation but who

made the observation, when, using what instrument, and so on.

■ Record daily attendance, including times of arrival and departure.

Recording medical information could be one process for a clinic or hospital where the word project above might involve several projects for each area within the hospital.

It could also be multiple processes, one for each area within the hospital where each process might be one procedure (Table 4.1).

It could also be multiple processes, one for each area within the hospital where each process might have multiple procedures (Table 4.2).

Of course, some of the procedures might be the same or very similar between units.

It is up to your organization to determine the definitions of these procedures. These procedures will form the specifications and requirements for the quality management of the observation process and for the computer systems.

When you are executing a process it is very important to understand the products produced. It might be an interesting exercise to ask those involved to describe the products being produced.

Table 4.1   Single Procedure Process

Process—Record Patient Information
Procedure 1 – Cardiac Unit
Procedure 2 – Pediatric Unit
Procedure 3 – Geriatric Unit
- - - -
- - - -
Procedure X – Special Unit

Time

Table 4.2   Multiple Procedures per Process

Process—Hospital Units
Process 1—Pediatrics
Procedure 1—Record Demographics Procedure 2—Record Urine Specimen Other Procedures
Process 2—Geriatrics
Procedure 1—Record Demographics Procedure 2—Record Blood Specimen Other Procedures
Process 3—Allergies
- - - -
- - - -
Procedure—Special Unit
Process X –
- - - -

Time

If there is not absolute agreement on what the products are then there is the potential for large problems.

As you can see above in some cases the project continues to exist after the procedures are put in use. This is to provide continued support and perhaps change control, which is also a relatively large issue with quality processes.

In some cases, the project part ends and any support, maintenance, or change control is covered with the procedures or as a separate project that continues.

How you decide to structure the work described here will depend on your company's best practices, the applicable regulations, your products, and your organization. The point should be that your organization has to sit down and decide how these various terms are implemented.

Requirements for ISO 9000 Documentation

Table 4.3 lists terms and definitions taken from ISO 9000:2005.

Table 4.4 shows how these documents might be used for data management.

It is vital that you take this and modify to match the processes you have adopted.

ISO 9000 Required Documentation

The following table of documentation uses three terms that need some clarification to interpret what follows. These terms are

Review
Verify
Validate

Table 4.3   ISO 9000 Documentation—Appendix A

Terms	ISO 9000:2005 Clause	Definition
Document	3.7.2	Information and its supporting medium.
Procedure	3.4.5	Specified way to carry out an activity or a process. (Note: Procedures can be documented or not.)
Quality Manual	3.7.4	Document specifying the quality management system of an organization
Quality Plan	3.7.5	Document specifying which procedures and associated resources shall be applied by whom and when to a specific project, product, process, or contract.
Record	3.7.6	Document stating results achieved or providing evidence of activities performed.
Specification	3.7.3	Document stating requirements.

Table 4.4   ISO 9000 Documentation—Appendix A

Terms	Definition—From ISO	Data Management Definition
Document	Information and its supporting medium.	Information prepared as part of the procedures used.
Procedure	Specified way to carry out an activity or a process. (Note: Procedures can be documented or not.)	A specified way to carry out an activity or a process to obtain the required medical information.
Quality Manual	Document specifying the quality management system of an organization.	Quality manual will specify the quality management system.
Quality Plan	Document specifying which procedures and associated resources shall be applied by whom and when to a specific project, product, process, or contract.	The project plan will specify any activities or responsibilities that are quality-specific. The procedures used to execute the steps in the plan should indicate any quality related activities.
Record	Document stating results achieved or providing evidence of activities performed.	The project plan will specify the deliverables or products of each step in the plan. These will include the records that are evidence that activities were performed.
Specification	Document stating requirements.	This document(s) will describe what information is collected and how it is collected.

They are used to describe what happens to some of the documentation required by ISO 9000.

The usage of these terms are as follows:

Review a document. This implies that document is reviewed, almost stand-alone, to see whether it meets the specifications for that document.

Verify a document. This is to verify that the document contains the information it is supposed to. For example, if this is a design document, it should describe the design of certain requirements. To verify the design document is to see whether it covers the necessary requirements.

Validate a document. This is to confirm that the document did, in fact, produce the results it was supposed to. For example, to validate a design document would involve validating that the design described in the document was actually implemented.

Another word that needs some clarification is the term *requirements*. In the ISO 9000 this word refers to any kind of documentation that is needed as part of your processes. In systems development, the term *requirements* normally refers to user requirements or design requirements or something else that is needed by the system.

Records Required for ISO 9000

The following annex is from ISO 9001:2008 (Table 4.5).

It is possible to show where these documents can be produced as the medical information is observed (Table 4.6).

Table 4.5 SDLC Version of Documents Required by ISO 9001:2008—Appendix B

Clause	Records Required
5.6.1	Management reviews
6.2.2 e	Education, training, skills, and experience
7.1 d	Evidence that the realization processes and resulting product fulfil requirements
7.2.2	Results of the review of requirements related to the product and actions arising from the review
7.3.2	Design and development inputs relating to product requirements
7.3.4	Results of design and development reviews and any necessary actions
7.3.5	Results of design and development verification and any necessary actions
7.3.6	Results of design and development validation and any necessary actions
7.3.7	Results of the review of design and development changes and any necessary actions
7.4.1	Results of supplier evaluations and any necessary actions arising from the evaluations
7.5.2 d	As required by the organization to demonstrate the validation of processes where the resulting output cannot be verified by subsequent monitoring or measurement
7.5.3	The unique identification of the product, where traceability is a requirement
7.5.4	Customer property that is lost, damaged, or otherwise found to be unsuitable for use
7.6 a	Basis used for calibration or verification of measuring equipment where no international or national measurement standards exist

(Continued)

Table 4.5 (*Continued*) SDLC Version of Documents Required by ISO 9001:2008—Appendix B

Clause	Records Required
7.6	Validity of the previous measuring results when the measuring equipment is found not to conform to requirements
7.6	Results of calibration and verification of measuring equipment
8.2.2	Internal audit results and follow-up actions
8.2.4	Indication of the person(s) authorizing release of product
8.3	Nature of the product nonconformities and any subsequent actions taken, including concessions obtained
8.5.2 e	Results of corrective action
8.5.3 d	Results of preventive action

Standard Operating Procedures (SOPs)

When it comes to demonstrating quality, SOPs play a vital role. They describe what must be done and what is produced. This forms the basis of determining that what was supposed to be done was done.

Usually Required SOPs

Security and access to facility
Security and access to computer system

SOP(s) Covering a Visit (Might Be Separate SOPs)

- Scheduling
- Filling out information if paper, eCRF if eDC
- Taking and handling samples
- Administering drug or other treatment
- Use of equipment for some observations, e.g., X-rays, MRI, ECG
- Maintenance of equipment

Table 4.6   ISO 9000 Documentation—Appendix A

Clause	Records Required	SDLC Documentation
5.6.1	Management reviews	
6.2.2 e)	Education, training, skills, and experience	Have training records for all involved in observing the information. This can be a file for each employee with a resumé or summary of a resumé and a training log (template attached) listing additional training.
7.1 d)	Evidence that the realization processes and resulting product fulfill requirements	This can be a table that summarizes the various requirements documents and then the corresponding documentation showing the requirements are met.
7.2.2	Results of the review of requirements related to the product and actions arising from the review	This could be covered in a detailed plan showing all documents, reviews, and approvals.
7.3.2	Design and development inputs relating to product requirements	Should be contained in the specifications. It might be necessary to include a summary.
7.3.4	Results of design and development reviews and any necessary actions	This can be applied to nearly all documentation; however, it certainly can be applied to the specifications, and the procedures. All documentation can be reviewed. The specifications can be validated against the actual results.
7.3.5	Results of design and development verification and any necessary actions	
7.3.6	Results of design and development validation and any necessary actions	

(*Continued*)

Table 4.6 (*Continued*)   ISO 9000 Documentation—Appendix A

Clause	Records Required	SDLC Documentation
7.3.7	Results of the review of design and development changes and any necessary actions	Change Control Procedures will document changes and any necessary actions.
7.4.1	Results of supplier evaluations and any necessary actions arising from the evaluations	Any changes from suppliers will be included in the change control process.
7.5.2 d)	As required by the organization to demonstrate the validation of processes where the resulting output cannot be verified by subsequent monitoring or measurement	N/A
7.5.3	The unique identification of the products, where traceability is a requirement	Major area where traceability is a requirement to trace the specifications from inception through completion.
7.5.4	Customer property that is lost, damaged, or otherwise found to be unsuitable for use	N/A
7.6 a)	Basis used for calibration or verification of measuring equipment where no international or national measurement standards exist	All instruments used for medical purposes must have standards (GLP).

(*Continued*)

Table 4.6 (*Continued*)   ISO 9000 Documentation—Appendix A

Clause	Records Required	SDLC Documentation
7.6	Validity of the previous measuring results when the measuring equipment is found not to conform to requirements	User must manage all instrumentation used (GLP).
7.6	Results of calibration and verification of measuring equipment	User must manage all instrumentation used (GLP).
8.2.2	Internal audit results and follow-up actions	Internal audits will be performed and the necessary reporting will be completed.
8.2.4	Indication of the person(s) authorizing release of product.	Documented in the release phase of the information.
8.3	Nature of the product nonconformities and any subsequent actions taken, including concessions obtained	This will be covered by the Change Control Procedure.
8.5.2 e)	Results of corrective action	This will be covered by the Change Control Procedure.
8.5.3 d)	Results of preventive action	This will be covered by the Change Control Procedure.

Common SOPs

Training—General recording of training
SOP on SOPs

Entry Procedures

Training on obtaining the values
There might be several SOPs for each of the different sets
of data

Demographic
Lab
Cardiovascular
Others

Computer Systems

Installation of new versions—could be several
Change control
Event (error) reporting
Training on use of the system

Potential Sources of These Procedures

It might look like a large task to produce the above procedures for all departments of a large hospital. There are, however, several potential sources for these procedures.

If you are implementing a new EMR/EHR computer system you might check with the vendor and see whether they have a users group. Most of these procedures are noncompetitive and very usable drafts of the procedures could be developed by an independent group and then shared. If there is no user's group you might consider a medical school. Developing drafts of these procedures might be an excellent research project for a medical school.

If your hospital is part of an Accountable Care Organization (ACO), it might be possible to organize a small group of representatives from the other hospital and have them develop the procedures.

Each hospital has an IRB and some IRBs work for more than one hospital. They might be a good organization to assist with procedures.

The Quality SDLC

The first step should be to fill out the matrix in Table 4.7 to show how the procedures that are adopted work. This matrix should contain a lot of detail or references to the detail.

Table 4.7   SDLC Plan Matrix

Phase	Procedures	Responsibilities	Products	QA Activities
Plan				
Requirements				
Development				
Testing				
Release				
Support				
Archival				

It should be possible to discuss the QA activities that will go on at each step and who will perform them.

The idea is to show how quality is being considered along the way. It should be possible to fill out the matrix shown in Table 4.7 for our procedures to collect the medical information.

Table 4.8 gives general examples of how the documentation might be structured. Obviously, it could be very different for some systems. Large complex systems might have a subset of this information for each module in the system. There might be a set of documentation like this for each diagnostic unit in the system.

Typically the procedures are kept short and concise. This makes them easier to execute, maintain and do the training (Table 4.8).

A version of this table that emphasizes the quality contributions should be placed in the quality manual.

Change Control

It is worth looking in detail at your Change Control Procedure(s). There are those who will argue that most errors occur when things change.

Table 4.8 Sample Plan Documentation

Phase	Procedures	Responsibilities	Products	QA Activities
1. Plan	PR-01—Version Plan	Version Lead Medical Lead Nurse Lead Lab Lead	Plan for Version nn.m	Review the plan. Does it address quality issues?
2. Requirements	PR-02—Development of processes to be implemented	Version Lead Medical Lead Nurse Lead Lab Lead	SRS for Version nn.m	Review the document to see whether it addresses quality requirements such as patient safety.
3. Development	PR-03—For each process, prepare draft of procedures (SOPs)	Version Lead Medical Lead Nurse Lead Lab Lead.	Draft Procedures Training Material	Do inspections of procedures. Consider the quality.
4. Test the Procedures	PR-04—Preparation of Test Scripts Execution of Test Scripts Closely monitor results for safety	Version Lead Medical Lead Nurse Lead Lab Lead	Test Plan Test Scripts Test Results	Study the traceability matrix for errors or omissions. Was quality considered in the coverage? Review some of the tests.

(Continued)

Applying the Organization to Observation Processes ■ 35

Table 4.8 (*Continued*)   Sample Plan Documentation

Phase	Procedures	Responsibilities	Products	QA Activities
5. Release	PR-05 — Preparation and execution of release instructions and documentation	Version Lead Medical Lead Nurse Lead Lab Lead	New Version — All Procedures Release Note	Do an audit of the quality aspects before it is released.
6. Support, Change Control	PR-06a — Problem Reporting PR-06b — Change Control	Version Lead Medical Lead Nurse Lead Lab Lead	Problem Reports Audit Reports	Audit the Change Control Procedure. Conduct regular meetings to study the quality aspects of the procedures.
7. Archival	PR-09 — Storage and retrieval of archived information	Version Lead	Archival records Test of archival records	Audit the archival procedure.

Typically, a representative group of hands-on personnel will form a Change Control Board (CCB). If your system has a users' group, it might be good to include a couple of users on the CCB. This group will oversee all changes.

A system should be set up to record all reported changes. These reported changes can be reviewed to see whether they really represent a change or whether the person reporting the change did not understand the operation. This might point to an area where there needs to be more training or more documentation, but might not represent a real change.

The changes then would all be reviewed by the CCB and given a priority and scheduled in a later release of the system. There might be an emergency problem that, for example, makes the system unusable and needs to be repaired as quickly as possible.

In any case, the operation of the CCB needs to be documented and any necessary procedures written and followed.

Personnel

The various personnel in the group that develops the computer systems might be something like the following. You should have a table similar to Table 4.9, which shows the staff.

Table 4.9   Resources Involved in the Systems Development and their Responsibilities

Position Title	Responsibilities	Signatures

The Quality Organization

Each organization needs specific staff who are assigned quality responsibilities. They will typically be asked to review all of the things going on for quality influences. In a large enough organization, these might be full-time positions. They are often referred to as the Quality Assurance Unit (QAU). They report outside of the users group, often to the finance department or other such group.

The idea is that you cannot QA your own work. This assures that they are not answerable to the groups they are QA-ing.

In a small organization, the QAU might be part-time staff. The key is to assure they are not QA-ing their own work.

The QA organization will be one of the main topics described in the quality manual.

Another part to the QA organization might be those activities that are regularly performed to improve quality. Are there meetings where the question, *Is there a better way?* Is routinely asked? Are there any activities that are executed with the goal of looking for a better way?

Other Related Processes

There are other processes that will become relevant to implementing computer systems. At a minimum, there will be procedures that the user has that might not appear to be relevant but in fact can be very important.

Take the case of seeing patients and recording their medical information. Looking at it from a process view, there is a tendency to separate the computer systems from the using of the computer system. We could argue that the process starts when we have a value ready to enter into the computer. In fact, the accuracy and integrity of that observation is not only a function of what happens after it is entered into the computer, but also what was done to observe the observation before it was entered into the computer.

Remember, the treatment of the patient and the accuracy and integrity of the data *starts when the patient walks in the door.*

What if everything that goes on to get the observation also had quality management applied to it?

What are all of the processes used to observe the observation? It is likely that there are some instruments used to make that observation. Are the instruments working properly? There is a good chance the instruments also contain a computer system.

It is important to stand back and look at the big picture. This is an important aspect to determining the scope of the processes but, as you will see, it is also an important aspect to quality.

Chapter 5

Applying Quality Management to Computers

Purchaser or Developer

When reviewing the information in this section it is very important to consider whether you are a developer of one of these systems or a purchaser.

If you are the developer then you should consider everything that is presented here as something you should be doing.

If you are the purchaser of one of these systems then you have the responsibility to determine which of these procedures the vendor did and whether they were adequate.

Computer Systems

Almost all computer systems are developed using a Systems Development Life Cycle (SDLC) or Systems Life Cycle (SLC).

There are a variety of SDLCs that can be used. These are based on many things, including:

- The size and complexity of the application
- The tools used to develop the system
- The interfaces with other systems
- The interfaces with any instruments
- The criticality and importance of the system

A basic SDLC will have the following steps or phases:

1. Plan
   It is good to have a plan for this work. The ISO will require signatures and approvals of most of the products your process produces. It is wise to have a plan that describes what goes on at each step, what is produced, and who is responsible. Are specific quality actions taken, and other information, such as time and cost?

2. Specifications
   Any system that requires quality management will require documentation that describes what the system is supposed to do and how it will accomplish that. The system's intended function must be documented. Most SDLCs will produce this documentation at the beginning, before any development has begun. There are some newer processes that will develop these specifications as the system is being developed.
   The key is, before the system is put into use, can you demonstrate that the system performs as it is required?
   The specifications can go by several names such as user requirements, functional requirements, system requirements, design, design specifications, and so on.
   The format and structure of some of this information may depend on the tools being used to develop the system. The structure and content of the design documentation, for example, will likely have a certain

structure that depends on the underlying database system being used.

3. Development

Obviously the steps in this part of the process will depend on the tools being used to develop the system. Typically, the key to this part of the SDLC will be development rules or conventions. Are there recommendations regarding file sizes or file naming conventions? Are there recommendations regarding the structure and size of the programs being written?

A common tool to assure compliance to these rules is a technique called *code inspections*. Here, a programmer who did not write the code will sit down with the programmer who did write the code and go line by line through at least some of the code to see that proper conventions were followed.

4. Testing

With a large system, testing can take on a variety steps. There is one key concept that is very important about testing. That is, when you are testing, you are always testing *against* something. The key is that this should not be what is in one's head. It must be something that is documented.

Typically, this should be what is in the specifications above.

Normally, the testing phase is where the product is tested against the specifications from Step 2 above. There is usually a document called a *traceability matrix*. This document lists the test name or ID for each test and then lists the name or ID of the specification that the test tests. It will also include the result of the tests—pass/fail— and should include a reference of what to do if the test failed.

Note: when the specifications are written, it is usually recommended that they be short and concise— perhaps only one or two sentences. Avoid long flowing paragraphs of prose because it can be very difficult to test. As a matter of fact, it can be a good practice to ask how you would test a specification as the specifications above are being written. If a particular specification sounds difficult to test, the specification may need to be rewritten.

There will likely be some activities that would be considered testing in other phases. For example, there is often some testing done during the development phase. It is usually referred to as debugging and is often not well documented. This is typically satisfactory because the testing being done there will be repeated later during the formal testing.

It can also be the case that the testing group will not accept a new version for testing unless it can pass a set of basic capabilities. If the testing group begins testing the system and finds there are some basic errors that will not let them execute certain modules, it can be a waste of their time to try running tests.

It is also the case that once the system is released, the users will be testing the system in their environment before they turn it over for production use.

Whatever the testing processes are, they need to be documented and any resulting evidence to show the system is performing correctly must be reviewed and approved.

5. Release

It is a good idea to document the official release of a version for usage. It is important because it represents a change in responsibilities for the version and therefore the results of using that version. Therefore, the release of a version should include something that clearly states the date of the release. It will also typically include the directions on how to install this new version, including any data migration tasks, changes in usage procedures, and additional training required on the part of the users.

6. Usage

This is the phase that begins after the new version is installed and is being used in production.

Given all procedures are updated and the users are retrained, perhaps the biggest issue in this phase is change control. This can include reporting any events that might look like a bug. Not all events reported as bugs turn out to be bugs. The user might report it as a bug but in fact, the user may have misunderstood the system.

It is necessary to have a mechanism for reporting these events and then following up on them to get closure, whatever that might be.

7. Archival

In some environments where medical information is managed, it might be a requirement to back up old versions of either the software, the data, or both. It would, of course, be necessary to store it in such a way that it can be easily retrieved at a later date.

It would also be necessary to determine how often or under what conditions it would need to be backed up.

Example SDLCs

Institute for Electrical and Electronic Engineers (IEEE) Software Engineering Standards

The IEEE standards have used an SDLC, shown in Table 5.1, for examples in some of their standards.

There can be some obvious changes to this like cycle, for example:

1. Functional Specifications

If the system is large or complex, it may not be as simple as going directly from requirements (what to do) to design (how to do it). It may require an analysis step in between. This is often called functional analysis.

Table 5.1   IEEE Software Life Cycle

Step or Phase	Description
Planning	Develop a plan.
Requirements	Create specifications for what the system is supposed to do.
Design	Create specifications for how the system is supposed to perform.
Construction	Develop the system using programming standards.
Testing	Test the system against the specifications above. This is usually done with a traceability matrix that lists each requirement and each design step with the name of the test script next to each.
Release	Provide documentation for the release and installation of the system in the users' productions environment. This must include changes to procedures, additional training, and data migration, or other activities required by the change.
Use	Support the user with user documentation, training, and change control when the system is changed or updated.
Archival	Store data and documentation for later reference.

2. Combining Steps or Phases

   On the other hand, if the system is simple or you are using a high-level language such as Excel or SAS, the design may be very simple and some simple text included in the requirements might also cover the design.

3. Testing

   The testing might be divided into more than one step. For example, it is not uncommon to do functional or black box testing. This is testing that simply tests the user interface.

Structural or white box testing looks at the inside of the system, at some of the design features, and tests those.

Production testing is testing in the user's environment, usually after the system is released, although, there can be cases where some of the users agree to test versions of the system that are not released yet. This is called beta testing.

The key to testing is to remember that you are always testing *against something*. You can't just test. The question is: *what do you have to test against?* Obviously, this is one reason for specifications. The testing should show that the specifications are met.

Another key activity to watch during testing is coverage. That is, how many of the requirements and designs are you testing? How much of the system did you cover?

Medical Device Software Standard IEC 62304

This international standard [4] provides a lot of information regarding the development of regulated software. Even though this software is considered non-regulated, some of the suggestions here can be very useful. The SDLC they use can also be found in other documents:

1. Software Development Planning
2. Software Requirements Analysis
3. Software ARCHITECTURAL Design
4. Software Detailed Design
5. Software UNIT Implementation and Verification
6. Software Integration and Integration Testing
7. Software SYSTEM Testing
8. Software Release

Other Example SDLCs

Likewise, the Project Management Institute (PMI) also has methods for developing an SDLC, Carnegie Mellon Institute has an SDLC, and there are other sources as well.

EHR Specifications

Perhaps the most important information when developing a computer system is the development of documentation indicating the system's intended function. These are often called the system specifications or requirements.

Given the situation where our systems record and manage patient health information and that information is used to treat the patients, it is important that the information has a certain level of accuracy and integrity. Obviously, there can be some information that is more important than others and therefore might need extra attention when developing and supporting the system.

In the end we want to be able to demonstrate the system fulfills its intended function and quality attributes.

The HealthIT organization has prepared a document: FDASIA. This document has undergone public review and is currently available on the FDA docket as **FDA-2014-N-0339—Proposed Risk-Based Regulatory Framework for Health Information Technology Report.**

In this document, it is proposed that the specifications in the computer system can be grouped into one of three categories:

    I. Administrative Health IT Functionality
   II. Health Management Health IT Functionality
 III. Medical Device Health IT Functionality

One of the assumptions is that the specifications that are level I need little or no verification of their functionality. Those that are level II can have the level of verification that most companies are currently providing. Those in level III are important information and should be treated as though they were a device and require the same level of verification by FDA for medical device approvals.

   ■ *A more detailed description of the three categories can be found in Appendix B of this document.*

Applying Your Quality Management System

A quality management system is simply the quality organization you have, the responsibilities of each part of it, along with names of the managers of the various functions that deliver the desired quality. It will include the quality control and quality assurance procedures used to ensure the desired level of quality. It should show how each person has the opportunity to positively influence the quality of what is done.

If we look at ISO 9000, it calls for specific activities for the documentation.

Requirements for ISO 9000 Documentation

The following terms and definitions are taken from ISO 9000:2005 (Table 5.2).

Table 5.2   ISO 9000 Documentation—Appendix A

Terms	ISO 9000:2005 Clause	Definition
Document	3.7.2	Information and its supporting medium
Procedure	3.4.5	Specified way to carry out an activity or a process Note: Procedures can be documented or not.
Quality Manual	3.7.4	Document specifying the quality management system of an organization
Quality Plan	3.7.5	Document specifying which procedures and associated resources shall be applied by whom and when to a specific project, product, process or contract
Record	3.7.6	Document stating results achieved or providing evidence of activities performed
Specification	3.7.3	Document stating requirements

Table 5.3 shows how these terms could be used in an SDLC.

It is vital that you take this and modify to match the SDLC you have adopted.

ISO 9000 Required Documentation

The following table of documentation uses three terms that need some clarification to interpret what follows. These terms are

Review
Verify
Validate

They are used to describe what happens to some of the documentation required by ISO 9000.

The usage of these terms are as follows:

Review a document. This implies that document is reviewed, almost stand-alone, to see whether it meets the specifications for that document.

Verify a document. This is to verify that the document contains the information it is supposed to. For example, if this is a design document, it should describe the design of certain requirements. To verify the design document is to see whether it covers the necessary requirements.

Validate a document. This is to confirm that the document did, in fact, produce the results it was supposed to. For example, to validate a design document would involve validating that the design described in the document was actually implemented.

Another word that needs some clarification is the term *requirements*. In the ISO 9000 this word refers to any kind of documentation that is needed as part of your processes.

Table 5.3 SDLC Version of Documentation

Terms	Definition	SDLC Definition
Document	Information and its supporting medium.	Information prepared as part of the procedures used.
Procedure	Specified way to carry out an activity or a process. (Note: Procedures can be documented or not.)	A specified way to carry out an activity or a process to produce the results specified in the SDLC.
Quality Manual	Document specifying the quality management system of an organization.	Quality manual specify the quality management system used in the SDLC.
Quality Plan	Document specifying which procedures and associated resources shall be applied by whom and when to a specific project, product, process, or contract.	The project plan will specify any activities or responsibilities that are quality-specific. The procedures used to execute the steps in the plan should indicate any quality related activities.
Record	Document stating results achieved or providing evidence of activities performed.	The project plan will specify the deliverables of each phase in the SDLC. These will include the records that are evidence that activities were performed.
Specification	Document stating requirements.	There will likely be several different types of specification documents. These documents will be clearly identified as well as those documents showing which requirements were met.

In systems development, the term *requirements* normally refers to user requirements or design requirements or something else that is needed by the system.

Records Required for ISO 9000

The following annex is from ISO 9001:2008 (Table 5.4).

It is also possible to show where these documents are produced in the SDLC (Table 5.5).

Table 5.6 shows the same documentation but tried to indicate the specific documents where this information is stored. It would be a necessary exercise for your organization to develop such a table for your SDLC.

Table 5.4   SDLC Version of Documents Required by ISO 9001:2008—Appendix B

Clause	Records Required
5.6.1	Management reviews
6.2.2 e	Education, training, skills, and experience
7.1 d	Evidence that the realization processes and resulting product fulfill requirements
7.2.2	Results of the review of requirements related to the product and actions arising from the review
7.3.2	Design and development inputs relating to product requirements
7.3.4	Results of design and development reviews and any necessary actions

(Continued)

Table 5.4 (*Continued*)   SDLC Version of Documents Required by ISO 9001:2008—Appendix B

Clause	Records Required
7.3.5	Results of design and development verification and any necessary actions
7.3.6	Results of design and development validation and any necessary actions
7.3.7	Results of the review of design and development changes and any necessary actions
7.4.1	Results of supplier evaluations and any necessary actions arising from the evaluations
7.5.2 d	As required by the organization to demonstrate the validation of processes where the resulting output cannot be verified by subsequent monitoring or measurement
7.5.3	The unique identification of the product, where traceability is a requirement
7.5.4	Customer property that is lost, damaged, or otherwise found to be unsuitable for use
7.6 a	Basis used for calibration or verification of measuring equipment where no international or national measurement standards exist
7.6	Validity of the previous measuring results when the measuring equipment is found not to conform to requirements
7.6	Results of calibration and verification of measuring equipment
8.2.2	Internal audit results and follow-up actions
8.2.4	Indication of the person(s) authorizing release of product.
8.3	Nature of the product nonconformities and any subsequent actions taken, including concessions obtained
8.5.2 e	Results of corrective action
8.5.3 d	Results of preventive action

Table 5.5 ISO 9000 Documentation—Appendix A

Clause	Records Required	SDLC Documentation
5.6.1	Management reviews	
6.2.2 e	Education, training, skills and experience	Have training records for all involved in the SDLC. This can be a file for each employee with a resumé or summary of a resumé and a training log (template attached) listing additional training.
7.1 d	Evidence that the realization processes and resulting product fulfill requirements	This can be a table that summarizes the various requirements documents and then the corresponding documentation showing the requirements are met.
7.2.2	Results of the review of requirements related to the product and actions arising from the review	This could be covered in a detailed plan showing all documents, reviews, and approvals.
7.3.2	Design and development inputs relating to product requirements	Should be contained in the specifications. It might be necessary to include a summary.
7.3.4	Results of design and development reviews and any necessary actions	This can be applied to nearly all documentation; however, it certainly can be applied to the specifications, the development, and then the testing. All documentation can be reviewed. The eesign documentation can be verified against the requirements, the specifications can be validated against the test results.
7.3.5	Results of design and development verification and any necessary actions	
7.3.6	Results of design and development validation and any necessary actions	

(*Continued*)

Table 5.5 (*Continued*)   ISO 9000 Documentation—Appendix A

Clause	Records Required	SDLC Documentation
7.3.7	Results of the review of design and development changes and any necessary actions	Change control procedures will document these changes and any necessary actions.
7.4.1	Results of supplier evaluations and any necessary actions arising from the evaluations	Any changes from suppliers will be included in the change control process.
7.5.2 d	As required by the organization to demonstrate the validation of processes where the resulting output cannot be verified by subsequent monitoring or measurement	N/A
7.5.3	The unique identification of the product, where traceability is a requirement	Major area where traceability is a requirement to trace the specifications from inception through complete testing. This will be documented with the traceability matrix that displays this tracing.
7.5.4	Customer property that is lost, damaged, or otherwise found to be unsuitable for use	N/A

(Continued)

Table 5.5 (*Continued*)   ISO 9000 Documentation—Appendix A

Clause	Records Required	SDLC Documentation
7.6 a	Basis used for calibration or verification of measuring equipment where no international or national measurement standards exist	All instruments used for medical purposes must have standards (GLP).
7.6	Validity of the previous measuring results when the measuring equipment is found not to conform to requirements	Outside the scope of the software vendor. User must manage all instrumentation used (GLP).
7.6	Results of calibration and verification of measuring equipment	Outside the scope of the software vendor. User must manage all instrumentation used (GLP).
8.2.2	Internal audit results and follow-up actions	Internal audits will be performed and the necessary reporting will be completed.
8.2.4	Indication of the person(s) authorizing release of product.	Documented in the Release phase of the SDLC.
8.3	Nature of the product nonconformities and any subsequent actions taken, including concessions obtained	This will be covered by the Change Control Procedure.
8.5.2 e	Results of corrective action	This will be covered by the Change Control Procedure.
8.5.3 d	Results of preventive action	This will be covered by the Change Control Procedure.

Table 5.6   Sources of Records Required by ISO 9001:2008

Clause	Records Required	Source of Record
5.6.1	Management reviews	QMS Manual
6.2.2 e	Education, training, skills, and experience	Personnel Files
7.1 d	Evidence that the realization processes and resulting product fulfill requirements	TM Report
7.2.2	Results of the review of requirements related to the product and actions arising from the review	TM Report
7.3.2	Design and development inputs relating to product requirements	SDLC Specifications
7.3.4	Results of design and development reviews and any necessary actions	SDLC Specifications and SOPs
7.3.5	Results of design and development verification and any necessary actions	SDLC Specifications and SOPs
7.3.6	Results of design and development validation and any necessary actions	TM/Release Report
7.3.7	Results of the review of design and development changes and any necessary actions	TM/Release Report
7.4.1	Results of supplier evaluations and any necessary actions arising from the evaluations	Supplier Audit Report
7.5.2 d	As required by the organization to demonstrate the validation of processes where the resulting output cannot be verified by subsequent monitoring or measurement	Release Report

(Continued)

**Table 5.6 (*Continued*)   Sources of Records Required by
ISO 9001:2008**

Clause	Records Required	Source of Record
7.5.3	The unique identification of the product, where traceability is a requirement	SDLC Specifications
7.5.4	Customer property that is lost, damaged or otherwise found to be unsuitable for use	N/A
7.6 a	Basis used for calibration or verification of measuring equipment where no international or national measurement standards exist	GLP Procedures
7.6	Validity of the previous measuring results when the measuring equipment is found not to conform to requirements	GLP Procedures
7.6	Results of calibration and verification of measuring equipment	GLP Procedures
8.2.2	Internal audit results and follow-up actions	Audit Report
8.2.4	Indication of the person(s) authorizing release of product.	Release Procedures
8.3	Nature of the product nonconformities and any subsequent actions taken, including concessions obtained	Release Report/ Procedures
8.5.2 e	Results of corrective action	Audit Report
8.5.3 d	Results of preventive action	Audit Report

The Quality SDLC

The first step should be to fill out the matrix in Table 5.7 to show how the SDLC that has been adopted works. This matrix should contain a lot of detail or references to the detail.

It should be possible to discuss the QA activities that will go on at each step and who will perform them.

The idea is to show how quality is being considered along the way. It should be possible to fill out the following matrix for our SDLC (Table 5.7).

The following table gives some general examples of how the documentation might be structured. Obviously, it could be very different for some systems. Large complex systems might have a subset of this information for each module in the system. There might be a set of documentation like this for each diagnostic unit in the system.

Typically the procedures are kept short and concise. This makes them easier to execute, maintain and do the training (Table 5.8).

Table 5.7   SDLC Plan Matrix

Phase	Procedures	Responsibilities	Products	QA Activities
Plan				
Requirements				
Design				
Development				
Testing				
Release				
Install				
Support				
Archival				

Table 5.8 Draft SDLC Plan

Phase	Procedures	Responsibilities	Products	QA Activities
1. Plan	PR-01—Version Plan	Version Lead Programming Lead User Lead	Plan for Version nn.m	Review the plan. Does it address quality issues?
2. Requirements	PR-02—Development of System Requirements Specification (SRS)	Develop or update the requirements	SRS for Version nn.m	Review the document to see whether it addresses quality requirements such as patient safety.
3. Design	PR-03—Development of System Design Specification (SDS)	Develop or update the design document	SDS for Version nn.m	Review the document for coverage of all quality aspects of the requirements.
4. Development	PR-04—Coding and naming conventions	Write the required code or update existing code based on Specifications—SRS and SDS.	Source Code Other files—Data, control, Help	Do code inspections. Consider the quality of the coding.

(Continued)

Table 5.8 (Continued)   Draft SDLC Plan

Phase	Procedures	Responsibilities	Products	QA Activities
5. Testing	PR-05a—Preparation of Traceability Matrix PR-05b—Preparation of Test Scripts PR-05c—Execution of Test Scripts	Test Group Lead Testers	Test Plan Test Scripts Traceability Matrix Test Results	Study the traceability matrix for errors or omissions. Was quality considered in the coverage? Review some of the tests.
6. Release	PR-06—Preparation of Release instructions and documentation	Version Lead Programming Lead	New Version—All files Release Note	Do an audit of the quality aspects before it is released.
7. Install	PR-07—Preparation of Installation Instructions	Customer Support	Installation Instructions Data Migration Update Documentation	Encourage users to sometimes audit the system before production use and after it goes into production.

(Continued)

Table 5.8 (Continued)   Draft SDLC Plan

Phase	Procedures	Responsibilities	Products	QA Activities
8. Support, Change Control	PR-08a—Problem Reporting PR-08b—Change Control	Customer Support Version Lead	Problem Reports	Audit the Change Control Procedure. Conduct regular meetings to study the quality aspects of the system use.
9. Archival	PR-09—Storage and Retrieval of Archived Information	Version Lead	Archival Records Test of archival records	Audit the archival procedure.

A version of this table that emphasizes the quality contributions should be placed in the *Quality Manual.*

Change Control

It is worth looking in detail at your Change Control Procedure(s). There are those who will argue that most errors occur when things change.

Typically a representative group of hands-on personnel will form a Change Control Board (CCB). If your system has a users' group, it might be good to include a couple of users on the CCB. This group will oversee all changes.

A system should be set up to record all reported changes. These reported changes can be reviewed to see whether they really represent a change or whether the person reporting the change did not understand the operation. This might point to an area where there needs to be more training or more documentation, but might not represent a real change.

The changes then would all be reviewed by the CCB and given a priority and scheduled in a later release of the system. There might be an emergency problem that, for example, makes the system unusable and needs to be repaired as quickly as possible.

In any case, the operation of the CCB needs to be documented and any necessary procedures written and followed.

Personnel

The various personnel in the group that develops the computer systems might be something like the following. You should have a table similar to Table 5.9, which shows the staff.

Table 5.9   Resources involved in the Systems Development and their Responsibilities

Position Title	Responsibilities	Signatures

The Quality Organization

Each organization needs specific staff who are assigned quality responsibilities. They will typically be asked to review all of the things going on for quality influences. In a large enough organization, these might be full-time positions. They are often referred to as the Quality Assurance Unit (QAU). They report outside of the system development group, often to the finance department or other such group.

The idea is that you cannot QA your own work. This assures that they are not answerable to the groups they are QA-ing.

In a small organization, the QAU might be part-time staff. The key is to assure they are not QA-ing their own work.

The QA organization will be one of the main topics described in the quality manual.

Another part to the QA organization might be those activities that are regularly performed to improve quality. Are there meetings where it is routinely asked, *"Is there a better way?"* Are there any activities that are executed with the goal of looking for a better way?

Purchased Systems

Most of the hospitals and clinics will be using EMR/EHR that they purchased. Whether or not the system is purchased, the documentation and practices outlined above for ISO 9000 still need to be done. The question will be, *does the vendor do it or does the purchaser do it?*

For systems like these, much of what is described here should be done by the vendor.

It is important that the purchasers of these systems verify the vendors' procedures. Do their procedures show quality?

This question is usually addressed by auditing the vendor.

If the vendor has a lot of users, auditing them can be very disruptive. It can also mean that when you go to do an audit, there are other companies also doing an audit.

If there is a users' group, it can be OK to form an auditing team that would go and do the audit for all members of the users' group who want this.

As the purchaser, you have the responsibility to audit the vendor as described above and you need have SOPs that describe your processes when the system is installed at your location(s), and then verify that it is working correctly.

There will also be some issues regarding how changes are implemented and communicated to users, as well as issues regarding security, archiving, and restoration of the medical information.

Chapter 6

The HIMSS-EHR Developer Code of Conduct

The EHR Developer Code of Conduct focuses on the following topics:

General business practices
Patient safety
Usability
Interoperability and data portability
Clinical and billing documentation
Privacy and security
Patient engagement

All of these topics form an outline for the specification for the EHR system.

The EHR Developer Code of Conduct indicates the importance of quality in the EHR systems and emphasizes the importance of using quality management principles in the implementation of these systems.

http://www.himssehra.org/ASP/codeofconduct.asp
http://www.himssehra.org/docs/EHR%20Developer%20
Code%20of%20Conduct%20Version%202%20Final.pdf

Chapter 7

Developing Standard Operating Procedures (SOPs)

As you might expect, there are some general rules for the development of SOPs that make it possible to manage these documents. Obviously, there can be exceptions to some of these but keep in mind what the text is recommending.

There is another reference [3] from the EPA on how to prepare SOPs that can be very helpful. They address some similar questions when documenting procedures.

Identifying the SOP

When an SOP is displayed, either on paper or on a screen, each page or screen should have a header or footer as shown in Table 7.1 to identify the specific SOP. This is important to the person executing the SOP but it is also important if the operator decides to print the page or the screen. This information will identify the specific SOP and step in the SOP.

Table 7.1   SOP Page Header

Company Seal	Title	ID: SOP-MM-nn
Effective Date ___/___/___	Approved by: Title:	Page 1 of 3

Title:	Have the complete, unique title for the SOP.
ID:	It is important to have a unique identifier for the SOP so that if it is referenced elsewhere there will be no question about identifying the correct SOP. Typically, the ID is made up of two parts. The first part is the unique identifier for the SOP, the second part is the version number of the SOP. This number is incremented each time the SOP is changed. The products of the SOP will have a date associated with them. It is vital to know the date of the product compared to the date of the SOP that produced it.
Approved by:	This should identify the person and their title that is responsible for the SOP.
Page numbering:	The page or screen number needs to be displayed with the total number of pages or screens in the SOP.

History of Revisions

It is important to identify the changes that have been made to the SOP over time. Any auditors and FDA inspectors believe that problems tend to occur when changes are being made. A table such as the following will typically appear on the first page or the last page of the SOP (Table 7.2).

Table 7.2   Revision History Record

Version	Date	Change	Approved
001-AA	mm/dd/yyyy	Original Version	Initials or sign

SOP Sections

There can be any number of different sections in an SOP depending on what the procedure is but the following should be in almost every SOP.

Scope and Purpose

These sections should describe what areas and practices the SOP applies to. This is vital because you do not want someone, including an auditor or inspector, to apply the SOP in an area where it is not intended.

References

As you prepare the steps in the procedure there will be cases where the steps are already documented in a user manual or other document (inputs). The question will come up as to whether you should copy and paste from the other document into the SOP.

It is usually better to simply reference the other document, including its version number or date. If the other document changes it might get complicated trying to reproduce the instructions in the SOP.

Therefore, it is usually a good idea to specifically list any related documents, including other SOPS that are referenced in the SOP.

Glossary of Terms

Include a list of terms or abbreviations used in the SOP. Again, this is to avoid any possible confusion. This might also be a place where you want to reference a list of abbreviations in another document. The issue will be, what is the best way to keep the list updated accurately?

Procedure

Of course, there needs to be a procedure section that lists the steps that are executed during the procedure.

Procedures can tend to be one of two types or one of two extremes. The first case might be a series of steps executed to produce a single product that is then used.

The other extreme is where a series of steps is executed where each step is similar. For example, if a client walks into a store, there might be series of steps each client goes through to obtain their desired product. Or, when a patient walks into a clinic or hospital they will be subjected to a series of tests. The series of tests and the order will depend on the particular symptoms and the results of earlier tests.

It is also often better to keep the steps short. Avoid writing long paragraphs to describe each step. One or two sentences for each step is probably best. If there needs to be a long explanation of what is to be done, it might be better to refer to another document and add a training step if necessary.

Products

The procedure needs to produce certain products. These are the quality records.

They might be other documents, for example, specification for developing and supporting a computer system. The product produced might be a cure. The steps to obtain the product can be very different and produce a list of products—different test results.

In any case, as mentioned earlier, be careful if the procedure doesn't produce any products.

Deviations

It is not unusual to find as you are executing the SOP that you need to deviate from it. There is some room for judgment when you find you need to deviate.

If it is necessary to change a few of the steps for some unanticipated reason, that could be classified as a deviation. If you get into it and the entire SOP needs to be changed, that is probably more than a deviation and should require more attention.

When you get into an SOP and find that a couple steps need to be changed, it is not a problem if the deviation is documented and approved.

For example, if the fourth step states to collect a urine specimen but you cannot for some reason, you should have a field somewhere, perhaps a comment field, where you can document that you could not complete step four, explain why, and have the action approved by someone.

What to do when a deviation occurs can either be documented in the SOP itself or in the SOP on SOPs.

Length AD Detail

In general, an SOP should be relatively short, that is, no longer than two to eight pages. If it is longer than eight pages it has been found that people won't really study them.

It is also a good idea to be careful about how much detail is included. Obviously, you want to have enough detail so the person can follow the procedure but the detail can be referred to instead of included in the SOP.

Often the detail will change and you need to be sure the reference is to the accurate version; however, it can be a hassle to get SOPs approved so you don't want to be in a situation where the SOPs need to be approved every other day.

To help this, some things to consider are

- Don't use people's names: use job titles.
- Don't reference specific file names.

Contents

As stated earlier, reference other documentation that describes the detail. In general, it is not good practice to cut and paste large sections of other documentation into the SOPs. The contents of the SOPs needs to be kept up-to-date. If you start cutting and pasting sections of other documents, over time, the maintenance can become problematic.

Reviews

Review the SOPs on a regular basis, perhaps once a year or after any organizational, content, or procedural changes that might impact the execution of the procedure.

SOP on SOPs

Have one SOP that describes the material listed above and how to produce them.

Chapter 8

Compliance

Presumably, by now, you have figured out that the processes and procedures (standard operating procedures [SOPs]) you have implemented reflect whatever requirements apply to your products.

Compliance is the ability to demonstrate that you are operating according to a set of requirements.

If we combine two principles, first the products and then the processes and procedures, we come up with the following:

- Identify the products that you produce that are covered by the requirements.
- Identify the processes used to produce those products and document the steps, including references to any documentation needed for the production.

Identify the records that are generated as the process is followed. If no records are produced, the process must be changed to produce some records of the progress.

Run the process and produce the product.

Periodically study the steps in the process, the records and product that are produced against what they are supposed to be in the documentation.

When a problem or difference is encountered, determine the impact and correct whatever needs to be corrected but also ask whether there is a better way.

Some things that *must* happen:

1. There must be documented processes.
2. There must be documented evidence (periodic deliverables) that the process was performed.
3. Document includes *Approved* and/or *Responsible for* entries.
4. The process must be periodically reviewed and if it is not as expected, there must be a correction or improvement step.
5. The products that are generated by the process must be periodically reviewed and if they are not as expected, there must be a correction or improvement step.

Living Quality

It should be clear that when reviewing documents to sign off or looking at the results of an audit, or just meeting to discuss the use of the system, the following types of questions should be asked:

■ Could this be done a better way?
■ Is there anything here that can negatively impact patient safety?
■ Was anything overlooked?
■ Are we doing the best we can?
■ Is there anything in the next step that could be done better?

- Was there anything in the previous step that could have been done better?
- Am I doing everything I can to improve quality?

Occurrences

You should be trying to set up your processes so that nothing unexpected happens. You should have a list of all the things you know could happen and be prepared to address any issues that may arise (risk management).

What if something happens that you hadn't thought of? Even when this happens you need a process for addressing it. As soon as it happens you go into risk management mode and must be prepared to manage or mitigate the risks.

Quality Assurance

An International Organization for Standardization (ISO) definition states that quality control is the operational techniques and activities that are used to fulfill requirements for quality.

The American Society for Quality (ASQ) uses the following definitions for Quality Assurance and Quality Control.

Assurance: The act of giving confidence; the state of being certain or the act of making certain.

Quality Assurance: The planned and systematic activities implemented in a quality system so that quality requirements for a product or service will be fulfilled.

Control: An evaluation to indicate needed corrective responses; the act of guiding a process in which variability is attributable to a constant system of chance causes.

Quality Control: The observation techniques and activities used to fulfill requirements for quality.

To summarize:

1. Compliance = Processes + Quality Assurance, by Everyone
   Compliance to corporate needs and regulations requires documented processes that are monitored to assure they are producing correct (high quality or known quality) products and problems are discovered and fixed.
   These processes are known and followed by everyone in the organization. Quality cannot be assigned to a focus group in the corner.
2. Processes 101 (Project Management)
   Develop the process that you will document that produces the product(s) you need.
3. Standard Operating Procedures (SOPs)
   Prepare documentation of the procedures that will be followed during the process. This should include what goes into the process, manuals, work instructions, other SOPs, and then what products and documentation the procedure produces.
4. Quality Assurance
   Study what the procedure is supposed to produce, what was produced, and whether it meets the predetermined specifications and quality attributes. If it does not, then prepare a Corrective and Preventative Action (CAPA) plan to fix the problem.

   In addition, continually ask whether this is the best that can be done. If it is not, then prepare a CAPA plan to change it.
   This includes documentation to support the process.

5. Risk Management
   Apply risk management to the various things (Events) in the CAPA that need to be fixed and take appropriate action based on the risk level.

Chapter 9

Conducting Audits

Obviously, one of the major activities required for compliance is to study what you produce and how you are producing it to see whether it meets predetermined specifications and quality attributes.

This is typically done by conducting an audit.

The general definition of an audit is a planned and documented activity performed by qualified personnel to determine by investigation, examination, or evaluation of objective evidence, the adequacy and compliance with established procedures, or applicable documents, and the effectiveness of implementation [5]. The term may refer to audits in accounting, internal controls, quality management, project management, water management, and energy conservation.

Auditing is defined as a systematic and independent examination of data, statements, records, operations, and performances (financial or otherwise) of an enterprise for a stated purpose. In any audit, the auditor perceives and recognizes the propositions for examination, collects evidence, evaluates the same and, on this basis, formulates a judgment, which is communicated through an audit report. The purpose is then to give an opinion on the adequacy of controls (financial and otherwise) within the audited environment, to evaluate and improve the effectiveness of risk management, control, and governance processes.

Audits

A lot of the work the quality assurance unit (QAU) does will involve some kind of audit. This is where differences are identified and documented for study and potential subsequent correction (Corrective and Preventative Action [CAPA]).

There are a variety of different audit types that could be used. Some of these are

Internal audit
Vendor audit
Qualification audit
Follow-up audit
For-cause audit
Product, process, procedural, and system audits
Supplier/contract manufacturer audit
Team audit

There are others. The point is, there should be a goal for the audit. What is the purpose for the audit?

Audit Planning Checklist

Objective: Audit Goals

Clearly state all goals or objectives of the audit. If possible, list specific questions that the audit is intended to answer. These are likely to be goals that address regulatory issues, various risks, or problems that have been reported (Table 9.1).

Table 9.1   Audit Goals and Objectives

Goals and Objectives	References (If Appropriate)

Abstract: Audit Overview

Summarize the plan for the audit. Indicate where you plan to conduct the audit and what procedures you plan to review. Also, for each procedure indicate the inputs to the procedures and the deliverables from the procedures you plan to consider.

If this is a first audit or the audit of a vendor, identify specific procedures and associated documentation may have to be the first step in conducting the audit because you may have to go to the audit site to obtain that information.

Specific Responsibilities: Roles unique to this specific audit.

Identify the persons involved in the audit and their specific responsibilities.

Audit Leader:

_____

Responsibilities:

_____

_____

_____

Audit Team:

_____

_____

_____

_____

_____

Responsibilities:

_____

_____

_____

_____

Organization Being Audited
Organization:

_____

_____

Responsibilities:

_____

_____

_____

_____

Audit Report

If there are other groups that conduct audits, you might see whether they have a format for audit reports that they recommend. It is often important to consider carefully what you put in the audit report. Generally, it is good to focus on the plan and only document findings related to the plan. If you find things that are outside the scope of this audit, it is probably worth some discussion as to how it is written up.

If it is a problem it should definitely be documented somewhere, probably in this audit report. However, if it raises some issues that are well outside the scope of this audit, it might be better to separate it and place the details in a separate report.

Report Content

The report should do two things:

1. Summarize the information above so it is clear who conducted the audit, the goals or purpose of the audit, and the group being audited. It should also indicate who the *Lead Auditor* is because they will be asked to sign the audit report.
2. Document the findings of the audit, including the severity of the findings grouped by *Major, Moderate,* and *Minor.* There is also typically a section for comments.

The findings are often displayed in a table such as shown in Table 9.2.

Report Follow-up

After the report is completed and delivered to the audited group, it would be good if there could be a follow-up report that indicates how each of the findings will be addressed (Table 9.3).

Table 9.2   Audit Findings

Finding No.	Major, Moderate, Minor, Comment	Observation	Response (Not Required for Comment)

Table 9.3   Audit Report Follow-up

Finding No.	Major, Moderate, Minor, Comment	Observation	Response (Not Required for Comment)	Proposed/Actual Completion Date (dd/mm/yyyy)	Responsible Person (Name)

Chapter 10

Risk Management

Risk Management in Practice

Today, quality management, along with project management and some regulations, requires a risk management component to address issues when something goes wrong. A big part of what is being done here is monitoring your process (quality assurance [QA]) to catch things that do not produce the desired result or could be improved. One way to approach the solution to these problems is to apply risk management.

One should ask, *what could happen (an event) that would prevent the procedure from producing the desired result?*

In other words, *what is the risk?*

In our context, *risk is an event* that has two characteristics:

1. The likelihood or probability that the event will occur
2. The severity of the event or how bad the reaction to the event will be

Note: There is a third property that needs to be addressed but will not be pursued here; that is, the probability that the event will be discovered. Although we do not address it here, it is something you will need to consider.

The likelihood and severity can both be specified as quantitative values or qualitative values. That is, they can have values, for example, from 1 to 20, 20 to 50, and 50 to 100, or they might have values such as mild, moderate, and severe.

Given that this is risk, what is risk management?

Risk management can have several steps and there are a variety of ways to define these steps.

For example, the document titled *NIST Special Publication 800–39 Managing Information Security Risk* states that risk management has four components:

1. Frame risk (i.e., establish the context for risk-based decisions)
2. Assess risk
3. Respond to risk once determined
4. Monitor risk on an ongoing basis using effective organizational communications and a feedback loop for continuous improvement in the risk-related activities of organizations

Similarly, a generic risk assessment process has been set out in *ISO standard 31000*. The guidance can be applied to any kind of risk by any kind of organization. Essentially, the steps can be as follows:

1. **Establish the context**—What is the environment?
2. **Identify risks**—Search for potential problems.
3. **Analyze them**—Do an analysis of severity and likelihood of occurrence.
4. **Evaluate**—Decide what to do in each case.
5. **Control/treat**—Determine what to do to keep from occurring if one could occur.
6. **Monitor/review**—Watch what happens. Improve?

The *Q9 Quality Risk Management—Guidance for Industry* lays out the following steps.

Responsibilities

Quality risk management activities are usually, but not always, undertaken by interdisciplinary teams.

Initiating a Quality Risk Management Process

Quality risk management should include systematic processes designed to coordinate, facilitate, and improve science-based decision-making with respect to risk.

Risk Assessment

Risk assessment consists of the identification of hazards and the analysis and evaluation of risks associated with exposure to those hazards.

1. What might go wrong?
2. What is the likelihood (probability) it will go wrong?
3. What are the consequences (severity)?

Risk Control

Risk control includes decision-making to reduce and/or accept risks. The purpose of risk control is to reduce the risk to an acceptable level. The amount of effort used for risk control should be proportional to the significance of the risk.

Risk Communication

Risk communication is the sharing of information about risk and risk management between the decision makers and others. Parties can communicate at any stage of the risk management process.

Risk Review

Risk management should be an ongoing part of the quality management process. A mechanism to review or monitor events should be implemented.

Looking at these alternatives there are really three general steps:

1. Establish the Environment
   Discuss (document) the general background, staffs, priorities, and other characteristics of the risk environment.
2. Risk Analysis
   Document the three characteristics mentioned above.
   – What event (risk) might happen?
   – What is the likelihood (probability) it will go wrong?
   – What are the consequences (severity)?
   Categorize this information into similar risks and then prepare ways to mitigate each category.
3. Risk Monitoring
   Establish procedures to prevent it from happening again. What are the next steps? How are the activities monitored in the future? How are these events communicated to those who need to know?

Based on your products, staff, procedures, and general environment, it might be necessary to group these steps differently. If you feel that would make it clearer and more certain, do not hesitate to regroup the steps.

For our purposes, looking at a computer system, we will focus on the second step—identifying the risks through proposing some kind of mitigation for each.

Therefore, consider the following:

■ Risk Analysis—the identification, assessment, and prioritization of risks
■ Risk Mitigation—the coordinated and economical application of resources to minimize, monitor, and control the probability and/or impact of the risk

Chapter 11

Risk Analysis

Risk analysis is the process of defining and analyzing the dangers to individuals, businesses and government agencies posed by potential natural and human-caused adverse events. One could prepare a risk analysis report that describes the results of the Risk Management so that appropriate steps could be taken to mitigate as much of the risk as possible or necessary.

In a quantitative risk analysis, an attempt is made to numerically determine the probabilities of various adverse events and the likely extent of the losses if a particular event takes place.

Qualitative risk analysis, which is used more often, does not involve numerical probabilities or predictions of loss. Instead, the qualitative method involves defining the various threats, determining the extent of vulnerabilities and devising countermeasures should an attack occur.

– TechTarget, http://searchmidmarketsecurity.tech-target.com/definition/risk-analysis

The first step is to consider what the risks are. In other words, what events could happen? Then, what is the likelihood and what is the severity—either numerically or qualitatively?

Develop scales for the likelihood and severity such as the following:

Severity—1. Very Severe; 2. Moderately Severe; 3. Somewhat Severe; 4. Mildly Severe

Likelihood—1. Very Likely; 2. Somewhat Likely; 3. Slightly Likely; 4. Not Likely

Given this, it is possible to build a table for a risk or set of risks.

Risk Name _____ (Table 11.1)

Now the goal is to place entries into the table that will indicate what actions to take to mitigate the risk for each level of severity and likelihood.

For Example,

Risk Name _____ (Table 11.2)

A =

B =

C =

The goal, then, is to document the procedure in each case. For example,

A = low likelihood and low severity. In these cases you might do nothing or do periodic manual checks of the products and processes.

C = high severity and high likelihood. You might decide we are going to change your procedures so that this combination is impossible or you might do 100% sampling of the products.

Table 11.1   Risk Severity and Likelihood

		Likelihood			
		1	2	3	4
Severity	1				
	2				
	3				
	4				

Table 11.2   Risk Severity and Likelihood (Example)

		Likelihood			
		1	2	3	4
Severity	1	A	A	B	B
	2	A	B	B	B
	3	B	B	B	C
	4	B	B	C	C

Risk Mitigation

Risk mitigation is a systematic reduction in the extent of exposure to a risk and/or the likelihood of its occurrence. It is also called risk reduction.

Risk Management

When looking at implementing computer systems one approach might be to tie the management of risks into the phases of the life cycle. In other words, we will look at risks that could occur during development up to and including user acceptance testing. Then we will look at risks that could occur during the support and maintenance phase, including change control, and then finally risks that could occur during the decommissioning phase.

Table 11.3   Risk Severity and Likelihood by Phase

Phase of Life Cycle _____

Risk Title	Risk Description	Likelihood or Probability of Occurrence	Severity or Impact of Occurrence

For each of those three phases, a table as shown in Table 11.3 can be built and populated by the project team.

Suppose a system tracks a patient's cholesterol levels and risks associated and the *person doing the entry enters the wrong value*. The risk will depend on which field is being entered and perhaps what the incorrect value is.

So, the risk might be that the subject/patient's name is entered incorrectly.

The likelihood could be not likely, could happen, or is likely. The severity could be no impact, minimal impact, some impact, or large impact (Table 11.4).

What to Do about the Risk

If you are still in the development or configuration phase (Table 11.5), it might be good to have something similar to the following:

A = Do nothing because it is unlikely to happen

B = Program edit checks such as range checks or verify patient is already entered

C = Program *pop-down* list of valid values, require second entry or second verification.

Table 11.4 Risk Severity and Likelihood by Procedure

Phase of Life Cycle _____

Risk Title	Risk Description	Likelihood or Probability of Occurrence	Severity or Impact of Occurrence
Name Entry	The Subject/ Patient's Name Is Entered Incorrectly.	Could Happen	Minimal Impact

Table 11.5 Risk Severity and Likelihood Values by Phase

		Severity			
		No Impact	Minimal Impact	Some Impact	Large Impact
Likelihood	Not Likely	A	A	B	B
	Could Happen	A	B	B	B
	Is Likely	A	B	B	C

If you are in the support and maintenance phase where the system cannot be changed, then the entries might be something similar to the following:

A = Do nothing because it is unlikely to happen
B = Take extra steps to increase accuracy such as *Double Key Entry*
C = Do 100% source data verification

If you are looking at another field, the tables above might still be usable. For example, consider the field *number of cigarettes smoked*. This is typically a quality of life question and is virtually impossible to verify.

In this case it might have risk values of could happen but no impact. If you are not working on a study of smoking habits, the risk analysis/mitigation would state, "Don't worry about this one."

In other words, the entries in the tables above indicate the action to take to manage the risk.

There are a few things to look for when using this method.

Is there one table that could be used for a group of risks? What if a field is missing? Is there a subset of fields that would all have the same properties for that risk?

Managing Risks

Moving on to the next step—managing the risks is the goal. When dealing with critical information such as medical information where patients are at risk, risks must be managed to make things as safe as possible for the patient.

This means that you should have a process in place to identify the risk (the event) if and when it occurs as well as the severity, and be able to mitigate the risk before it causes serious harm.

Chapter 12

If All Else Fails

I will say that from time to time I pray. I won't go into a lot of detail but there is a line in one of the prayers that goes:

"Save us from the Fires of Hell."

Now, that is probably not a bad plea regardless of your spiritual orientation, but I noticed at one point that I had replaced one of the words.

As you might guess from the previous chapters, virtually all the documentation mentioned exists in files of some kind. They might be paper or electronic or some combination. It turned out that the line I had actually been saying, probably for many months, was

"Save us from the <u>Files</u> of Hell."

After some thought, I decided this was probably a much better prayer anyway.

I guess if you are having trouble doing compliance, don't be afraid to ask for help, wherever that help might be.

Appendix A

Deming: Key Principles

Deming offered 14 key principles to managers for transforming business effectiveness. The points were first presented in his book *Out of the Crisis* (p. 23–24). Although Deming does not use the term in his book, it is credited with launching the Total Quality Management movement.

1. Create constancy of purpose toward improvement of product and service, with the aim to become competitive, to stay in business, and to provide jobs.
2. Adopt the new philosophy. We are in a new economic age. Western management must awaken to the challenge, must learn their responsibilities, and take on leadership for change.
3. Cease dependence on inspection to achieve quality. Eliminate the need for massive inspection by building quality into the product in the first place.
4. End the practice of awarding business on the basis of a price tag. Instead, minimize total cost. Move toward a single supplier for any one item on a long-term relationship of loyalty and trust.

5. Improve constantly and forever the system of production and service, to improve quality and productivity, and thus constantly decrease costs.
6. Institute training on the job.
7. Institute leadership (see Point 12 and Chapter 8 of *Out of the Crisis*). The aim of supervision should be to help people, machines, and gadgets do a better job. Supervision of management is in need of overhaul, as well as supervision of production workers.
8. Drive out fear, so that everyone may work effectively for the company. (See Chapter 3 of *Out of the Crisis*.)
9. Break down barriers between departments. People in research, design, sales, and production must work as a team, in order to foresee problems of production and usage that may be encountered with the product or service.
10. Eliminate slogans, exhortations, and targets for the work force asking for zero defects and new levels of productivity. Such exhortations only create adversarial relationships, as the bulk of the causes of low quality and low productivity belong to the system and thus lie beyond the power of the work force.
    a. Eliminate work standards (quotas) on the factory floor. Substitute with leadership.
    b. Eliminate management by objective. Eliminate management by numbers and numerical goals. Instead substitute with leadership.
11. Remove barriers that rob the hourly worker of his right to pride of workmanship. The responsibility of supervisors must be changed from sheer numbers to quality.
12. Remove barriers that rob people in management and in engineering of their right to pride of workmanship. This means, *inter alia*, abolishment of the annual or merit rating and of management by objectives. (See Chapter 3 of *Out of the Crisis*.)

13. Institute a vigorous program of education and self-improvement.
14. Put everybody in the company to work to accomplish the transformation. The transformation is everybody's job.

Appendix B

FDASIA Health IT Report

The Food and Drug Administration Safety and Innovation Act (FDASIA), Public Law 112-144, requires that the Food and Drug Administration, working with some other agencies develop a report that contains a proposed strategy and recommendations on an appropriate regulatory framework pertaining to health information technology. The FDASIA Health IT Report fulfills the Section 118 requirement.

It is recommended that this report be a source for some of your practices.

https://www.fda.gov/downloads/AboutFDA/CentersOffices/ OfficeofMedicalProductsandTobacco/CDRH/CDRHReports/ UCM391521.pdf

The following are extracted from that report and contain information that is directly applicable to our topic of Quality Management.

Administrative Health IT Functionality

Administrative functionalities, including but not limited to software intended to facilitate admissions, billing and claims processing, practice and inventory management, scheduling, general purpose communications, analysis of historical claims data to predict future utilization or cost-effectiveness, determination of health benefit eligibility, population health management, reporting of communicable diseases to public health agencies, and reporting on quality measures pose limited or no risk to patient safety. As such, the agencies recommend that no additional oversight of these types of products is necessary to protect patient safety and promote innovation.[34]

Health Management Health IT Functionality – II

Health management health IT functionalities (sometimes referred to as clinical software) include, but are not limited to the following:

- Health information and data management
- Data capture and encounter documentation
- Electronic access to clinical results
- Most clinical decision support[35]
- Medication management (electronic medication administration records)
- Electronic communication and coordination (e.g., provider to patient, patient to provider, provider to provider, etc.)

---

[34] Some existing federal laws and regulations, such as those addressing the confidentiality, privacy, and security of electronic patient health information, or those that apply to wireless communications Federal Communications Commission (FCC), are applicable to all 3 categories of health IT (including administrative health IT).

[35] Clinical decision support (CDS) provides health care providers and patients with knowledge and person-specific information, intelligently filtered or presented at appropriate times, to enhance health and health care. Because its risks are generally low compared to the potential benefits, the FDA does not intend to focus its oversight on most clinical decision support. The FDA, instead, intends to focus its oversight on a limited set of software functionalities that provide clinical decision support and pose higher risks to patients, such as computer aided detection/diagnostic software and radiation therapy treatment planning software. See Chapter 6 for additional details.

- Provider order entry
- Knowledge (clinical evidence) management
- Patient identification and matching

The agencies believe the potential safety risks posed by health management health IT functionality are generally low compared to the potential benefits and must be addressed by looking at the entire health IT ecosystem rather than single, targeted solutions. If such health management health IT functionality meets the statutory definition of a medical device, the FDA does not intend to focus its regulatory oversight on such functionality because the agencies' proposed strategy and recommendations for a risk-based framework for health management health IT, outlined in Chapter 5, can help to assure a favorable benefit-risk profile of these functionalities. Chapter 5 articulates specific proposed priority areas and potential next steps that could help more fully realize the benefits of health IT.

Medical Device Health IT Functionality – III

Health IT with medical device functionality[36] is currently the focus of the FDA's oversight. Examples include computer aided detection/diagnostic software, radiation treatment planning, and robotic surgical planning and control software. Office of the National Coordinator for Health IT (ONC) and

---

[36] Section 201(h) of the FD&C Act defines device as "an instrument, apparatus, implement, machine, contrivance, implant, in vitro reagent, or other similar or related article, including any component, part, or accessory, which is– ... intended for use in the diagnosis of disease or other conditions, or in the cure, mitigation, treatment, or prevention of disease, in man or other animals, or intended to affect the structure or any function of the body of man or other animals, and which does not achieve its primary intended purposes through chemical action within or on the body of man or other animals and which is not dependent upon being metabolized for the achievement of its primary intended purposes."

Federal Communications Commission (FCC) may have complementary activities in certain areas (e.g., interoperable data exchange between a medical device and EHR, use of wireless spectrum for wireless medical devices, etc.). The strategy and recommendations for a risk-based health IT framework do not propose the need for new FDA authorities or additional areas of oversight. The FDASIA Health IT Working Group did recommend that the FDA provide greater clarity related to several aspects of medical device regulation involving health IT, including:

1. The distinction between wellness and disease-related claims
2. Medical device accessories
3. Medical device clinical decision support software
4. Medical device software modules[37]
5. Mobile medical apps[38]

"Promote the Use of Quality Management Principles"

Quality management principles and processes, as part of a quality system, have been adopted and implemented by more than one million companies and organizations worldwide to improve quality, efficiency, safety, and reliability. The selective adoption and application of existing quality management

---

[37] Report of the Section 618 Regulations Subgroup – Summary. Available at: http://www.healthit.gov/FACAS/sites/faca/files/FDASIARegulationSummary901413.pdf.

[38] The FDASIA Workgroup final recommendations accepted and adopted by the ONC Health IT Policy Committee on September 4, 2013, stated that the "FDA should expedite guidance on Health IT software, mobile medical apps and related matters." On September 25, 2013, the FDA issued final guidance entitled, Mobile Medical Applications: Guidance for Industry and Food and Drug Administration Staff, available at http://www.fda.gov/downloads/MedicalDevices/DeviceRegulationandGuidance/GuidanceDocuments/UCM263366.pdf.

principles and processes to health IT has been advocated by the IOM, the FDASIA Workgroup, and numerous health IT stakeholders including developers, implementers, and users. Some, but not all, health IT developers and healthcare facilities already adopt quality management principles.

A number of different approaches to quality management exist; however, they share certain common, underlying principles. Quality management principles help to identify, prevent, track, and monitor safety hazards and to reduce risks. They can be applied throughout the product lifecycle to design and development activities, to implementation, customization, integration, upgrades, maintenance, and operations, as well as to surveillance, reporting, risk mitigation, and remediation. Importantly, quality management principles are flexible, scalable, and adaptable so organizations (e.g., health IT developers, healthcare facilities, etc.) can tailor the application of these standardized processes to their individual circumstances and needs. Ultimately, quality management principles and processes provide a quality framework for companies and organizations to ensure that their products and services consistently meet their customers' needs and requirements that risk management principles are applied to identify, evaluate, mitigate, and remediate hazards, and that overall quality is continually improved.

The judicious application of quality management principles and processes by health IT stakeholders can promote the safe design, development, implementation, customization, integration, and use of health IT while fostering an environment that promotes innovation and continual improvement. However, because health IT represents a broad spectrum of products and services, health IT developers and organizations must have flexibility to determine the necessity of individual quality elements and to tailor the development and implementation of quality management processes appropriate for their products and services.

As part of the 2014 Edition Standards and Certification Criteria final rule, ONC adopted two safety-related certification criteria for EHRs: one that focuses on the application of user-centered design to medication-related certification criteria and another that focuses on the quality management system (QMS) used during the EHR technology design. In general, the Agencies believe that additional value to health IT purchasers and users could be realized if greater transparency existed around the quality management principles that were applied in the design and development, customization and implementation, and post-deployment use of health IT.

Summary and Conclusion

The application of quality management principles, including a quality systems approach by health IT stakeholders, is necessary for the safe design, development, implementation, customization, and use of health IT. The Agencies will work with health IT stakeholders to identify the essential elements of a health IT quality framework, leveraging existing quality management principles and identifying areas where quality management principles can or should be applied. The Agencies view this strategy, rather than a formal regulatory approach, as the appropriate method for advancing a health IT quality framework.

The Agencies seek input on the following questions related to promoting the use of quality management principles in health IT:

■ What essential quality management principles should apply to health IT? How should they apply to different stakeholders and at different stages of the health IT product lifecycle?

■ How do we assure stakeholder accountability for adoption of quality management principles? Is there a role for a non-governmental, independent program to assess stakeholder adherence to quality management principles? Is there a role for government?

Appendix C

Sample SOPs

The following are some examples and templates to use for standard operating procedures (SOPs) and some other files you might need.

Your team should review these and then make the necessary modifications so that they match your environment, regulations, products, and procedures.

For example, if your organization specializes in the treatment of serious cancer patients, some of these documents might be changed to reflect that.

Standard Operating Procedure Template

Standard Operating Procedure

SOP-001	Title: SOP Template	Version: 00A
Effective Date	Approved by:	
Applies to:		Page 1 of 2

Approvals

Name/Signature	Date

Annual Review Date:	By:
Version	Summary of Changes

Standard Operating Procedure

SOP-001	Title: SOP Template	Version: 00A
Effective Date	Approved by:	
Applies to:		Page 2 of 2

Purpose
Describe the reason for the procedure and what products are produced.

Scope
Describe which areas and which practices are covered by this SOP and, if necessary, which areas are not covered.

Referenced Documents

Doc ID	Title	Date

Glossary/Definitions

Term	Definition

Procedure
Describe the process being documented in a step-by-step manner. Indicate where documentation that can be audited or inspected is produced.

Appendices
Attach or reference templates, or other documents that are used in the procedure. Include the word *SAMPLE* in the water mark or footnote.

Information Systems Training Record

Standard Operating Procedure

SOP-001	Title: Information Systems Training Records	Version: 00A
Effective Date	Approved by:	
Applies to:		Page 1 of 3

Approvals

Name/Signature	Date

Annual Review Date:	By:
Version	Summary of Changes

Standard Operating Procedure

SOP-001	Title: Information Systems Training Records	Version: 00A
Effective Date	Approved by:	
Applies to:		Page 2 of 3

Purpose
This SOP describes the method of documenting the training of personnel in this department.

Scope
Any personnel involved in computer systems that are covered by validation guidelines must have adequate training. The training may include both computer usage and familiarity with the application system.

Training Records
A file will be maintained for each employee that documents the training and qualifications of each employee. Each file will contain a CV of each employee's qualifications.

In addition, a list of all training received by each person in the department will be maintained in the same files (sample in Attachment A). It will be the responsibility of each person to describe the training they have received and the dates it took place since the date of the CV.

This list should be updated as soon as possible after each course, but in any event, once each year (by January 31) the secretary will distribute to each employee his or her training list for them to update for the previous year. This is to be completed within 30 days and returned to the department manager for approval.

Both the employee and the manager will initial each training course on the list and return the list to the files.

If a certificate or other documentation exists for the course, a copy should be included in the file but is not required.

Standard Operating Procedure

SOP-001	Title: Information Systems Training Records	Version: 00A
Effective Date	Approved by:	
Applies to:		Page 3 of 3

Attachment A; Training Record

Name _____

Proc. No.	Title	Required?	If Yes, Understand and Will Follow	Signature/ Date
	Change Control	☐ Yes ☐ No	☐ Yes ☐ No	
	Systems Development Life Cycle	☐ Yes ☐ No	☐ Yes ☐ No	
	Qualification of IT Systems	☐ Yes ☐ No	☐ Yes ☐ No	
	Qualification Master Plan	☐ Yes ☐ No	☐ Yes ☐ No	
		☐ Yes ☐ No	☐ Yes ☐ No	
		☐ Yes ☐ No	☐ Yes ☐ No	
		☐ Yes ☐ No	☐ Yes ☐ No	
		☐ Yes ☐ No	☐ Yes ☐ No	
		☐ Yes ☐ No	☐ Yes ☐ No	
		☐ Yes ☐ No	☐ Yes ☐ No	

Change Control

A change was made in the compliance area that could have an impact on change control. We have assigned a quality manager (QM) to every project. Last week we assigned a second QM to every project. The first manager is the primary QM. The second is for backup and to offer some cross-breeding of the projects.

The Information Technology Infrastructure Library (ITIL) standards and practices in other companies in this industry handle change control according to the following:

1. Changes vs. Incidents
   You do not start with a change. The process starts with an incident or event. Something happens that starts someone thinking. Incidents or events are reported and then some are elevated to a change. Not all incidents require a change.
2. Incidents or changes can be assigned a level.
   Incidents are typically classified into one of three or four different levels or severities. Something such as the following:
   a. Simple – This is not a change and can be addressed by simply logging the fact that it happened and then it will typically have a simple process to implement the incident. It might also be a planned incident and be covered by normal maintenance or other operation.
   b. Emergency – This is an event or incident that is severe enough to potentially shut down the operations. It will typically require immediate attention and some things may need to be changed immediately and then documented and tested after the fact.
   c. Two or three other classes of incidents where the severity is between the simple incident and the emergency. These changes require a change process to assure that the change is implemented according to compliance.
3. Change Control Board (CCB)
   The CCB is a small group of professionals familiar with the system and are assigned the responsibility of implementing changes in a manner that maintains the system's accuracy and integrity – qualification and validation.

The changes implemented in the compliance department last week lend themselves to implementing a Change Control Process that is consistent with regulations and things like ISO.

Standard Operating Procedure

Purpose
To have a procedure to assure that the regulatory status of infrastructure components and application systems is maintained as required.

Scope
This procedure covers all infrastructure components and application systems covered by regulations.

Change Control Board
The Change Control Board (CCB) for each system (project) will be made up of the project manager and the two quality managers assigned to that project.

Procedure
1. Change Control Board (CCB)
   Each system that is covered by this procedure will establish a CCB. This board will be made up of at least one person familiar with the component or system and one quality manager. Others may be added to the CCB based on the current needs. These changes will be approved by the CCB and the responsible stakeholders.
2. Incidents
   Incidents will be reported to the manager of the CCB. Incidents will be reported by the change management system Maximo (or Remedy). This system produces a report of all incidents.
   Incidents may also be reported directly to the manager of the CCB but must be in writing.
3. Logging of Incidents
   All incidents will be logged and each member of the CCB will be notified of each incident.
4. Simple Incidents
   The manager of the CCB will examine each incident and decide whether the incident is simple. If it is simple, it can be addressed by logging the details (where?) and the incident can be addressed with existing procedures.
5. Changes
   Incidents that are not simple are elevated to a change status. The CCB will document the type of changes using the Change Control Form (CCF) located in Appendix A.
6. Classification of Changes
   The changes will be classified into one of the following three classes:

a. Emergency – The change must be implemented immediately.
b. Normal – The change is relatively important and will be implemented in the next set of changes to the system.
c. Low Priority – The change is placed on the list of changes that will be implemented in a later release.

7. Compliance
The CCB will review all changes to assure that the system will maintain its compliance with required regulations.

8. Status Reporting
The CCB will periodically (monthly?) produce a status report indicating the status of all changes.

Appendix – Change Request Form

SOP on SOPs

Approved by

Title	Signature	Date ___/___/___

Annual Review Date:	By:

Document History

Doc No.	Version	Effective Date	Brief Description of Change
XXX###	00		Original Plan

Purpose
To describe the process by which SOPs are written and managed.

Scope
This SOP applies to all procedures within _____.

Definitions

IA	Internal Auditor
PL	Project Leader
Dir	Directors of QA Center, Computer Group, Biostatistics Group
SyD	Systems Developer
AppSp	Application Specialist
Bst	Biostatistician
Ed	Editor
SOP	Standard Operating Procedure

Person Responsible	Activity
	Document Generation
Dir	Identifies need for new SOP.
PL/SyD/ AppSp/Bst	Prepares draft in view of regulatory environment, each for their respective departments.
	Formats and edits draft according to the standard format (Attachment 1).
Ed	The standardized format includes use of a template with assignment of a number, correct page numbering, and use of standard abbreviations and definitions (Attachment 1).
	Maintains format template, abbreviations, and definitions list and appropriate version control.
	Document Review
PL/SyD/ AppSp/Bst	Circulates draft among relevant personnel (hereafter referred to as *reviewers*) in departments affected.
	Revises draft based on reviewers' comments.
	Recirculates revised draft to reviewers.
	Arranges meeting with reviewers to resolve open issues, if necessary.
	Provides signature as the preparer of the SOP at the approval stage.
	Document Approval
Dir	Reviews final draft of all SOPs and, if satisfied, provides signature. If not satisfied, returns the draft with comments to the preparer for revision and recirculation.

Document Distribution

IA   Distributes new and revised SOPs to all affected personnel once they have been approved and keeps a distribution list (Attachment 2).

By signing the distribution list, personnel declare they have received and understand the SOP and agree to perform their work accordingly.

Document Revision

IA   Coordinates annual review of approved SOPs. SOPs will be reviewed at least once per year, or more often as necessary, by a group of relevant personnel. When revisions are required, the above process for review, approval, and distribution of SOPs will be followed.

Records the date of the review or, when revisions have been made, a summary of the revisions on the cover sheet of the revised SOP.

Document Storage and Archival

IA   Keeps original hard copies and electronic files of new and revised SOPs in the QA Center Library. Archives superseded versions in a central location for at least two years after the end of the last study conducted or for as long as required by regulations.

References

1. Government Auditing Standards: 1994 Revision (Supersedes 149628 and superseded by GAO-03-673G) - OCG-94-4. Published: 1 June 1994. Publicly Released: 21 June 1996.
2. World Health Organization and Clinical and Laboratory Standards Institute. *Supplement to the Laboratory Quality Management System Training Toolkit, Module 16—Documents and Records*.
3. United States Environmental Protection Agency (EPA), EPA/600/B-07/001. Guidance for Preparing Standard Operating Procedures (SOPs), April 2007.
4. Medical Device Software Standard IEC 62304.
5. ©ISO This material is reproduced from ISO/TC 176SC 2/N 525R2 with permission of the American National Standards Institute (ANSI) on behalf of the international Organization of Standards. All rights reserved.

Index